What Should You Know About Your Appraisal Inspection?

And Should You Worry About It?

By Steven Boucher

Copyright © by U S Realty Consultants LLC

All rights reserved.

No part of this book can be reproduced, broadcast or disseminated in any manner without the express written consent of the author. If you have a PDF version, please do not share the book or link. The author request that all parties obtain and enjoy their own personal copy of the book.

ISBN: 978-1983595110

REALTOR® is a federally registered collective membership mark which identifies a real estate professional who is a Member of the National Association of REALTORS® and subscribes to a strict Code of Ethics.

All company names, franchises, symbols and trademarks used in this book are used for reference purposes only and those companies exclusively own their respective names, symbols and trademarks.

This book is intended for education and entertainment purposes, and to provide a general knowledge of the appraisal process and what to expect while an appraiser is on site at a home. This is not a comprehensive discussion of the entire appraisal process and the scope of work of an appraiser.

No client relationship is intended, formed, nor desired from your support and control of this book.

This book is not intended to take the place of a local real estate expert, tax professional, lender or attorney and some sections of the country may have different local practices and methods for the purchase, sale and refinancing of real property. Please seek professionals in your local area concerning your specific situation.

US Realty Consultants LLC
6 New Westminster Road
Hubbardston, MA 01452
HubAppraisal.com

Contents

What Should You Know About Your Appraisal Inspection?
And Should You Worry About It?. 5
First–some basic ground rules and housekeeping!. 6
What is an Appraisal?. 6
Never an Advocate!. 7
Market Value 8
Why is the Appraiser Coming?. 9
Type of Property 9
Who is the appraiser's client?. 10
Types of Financing 11
FHA/HUD financing. 11
Observation from the Neighborhood 11
Observation from the Street 12
The FHA is a Stickler for Peeling Paint. 13
Is it a private street or way? 16
Finally, Let's Go Inside 17
The Kitchen 18
The Bathroom 19
The Attic. 19
Let's Go into the Basement! 20
In conclusion, ... 23
Disclosures 25
RESOURCES 26
About the Author 27

What Should You Know About Your Appraisal Inspection?
And Should You Worry About It?

Ever since the start of the Great Recession of 2007 there have been many layers of new banking and appraisal regulations rolled out by the federal government. Millions of real estate appraisals have been submitted to the banks by appraisers. The government has dropped every one of them into one massive computer database. Big Brother and Big Data are here, and they are asking the appraisal industry for more data and information about each property than ever before.

My name is Steven Boucher and I have been around the real estate industry since the mid- 1980's. I am a real estate broker as well as a Certified Residential Appraiser in Massachusetts. What follows is a quick overview of what an appraiser does and what we look for when we evaluate a property.

Under certain conditions, real estate appraisers have been put in the unfortunate position of being the messenger of bad news. Depending on what the appraisal will be used for, the federal government has created—and is now enforcing—strict programs and oversight involving mortgage loans and appraisal data. There are serious new provisions involving all loans backed or secured by secondary market players such as the Federal National Mortgage Association, commonly known as Fannie Mae, The Federal Home Loan Mortgage Corporation, known as Freddie Mac, and the Federal Housing Administration, to name a few.

These new provisions force the original mortgage department that originated the loan to buy back the loan should any errors or missing documentation be found, even if it is found years later. The banks and lenders want nothing to do with loans coming back to bite them later on, so they have become very careful from the beginning of the loan process by tightening access to credit, conducting more verifications, requiring more paperwork and instituting a more in-depth appraisal inspection and report. The problem is that no one has explained to the public how they are now impacted by these new regulations and financing processes.

This quick read will give you a better understanding of what we appraisers do and what we are looking for when we visit a property. Knowing this will allow you to take steps early on and prevent any issues from occurring with your property appraisal.

If you find this book interesting or helpful I urge you to checkout my website HubAppraisal.com and sign up as a subscriber to the website and blog. You can contact me with questions or ideas by using the contact drop down box.

First—some basic ground rules and housekeeping!

The following three definitions and explanations are at the core of every appraisal.

What is an Appraisal?

As per the Uniform Standards of Professional Appraisal Practice (USPAP),

> *(Noun) An appraisal is the act or process of developing an opinion of value; an opinion of value.*
>
> *(Adjective) of or pertaining to appraising and related functions such as appraisal practices or appraisal services.*

The USPAP is basically the appraisers' ethical playbook and pretty much covers every angle and scenario of appraising a property. There are rules, directions and opinions that appraisers must follow based on the USPAP.

An appraisal is an opinion of value based on the best available and similar data at any given point in time.

An appraisal valuation report can be developed for a property using the data from this week, or retrospectively—let's say from five years ago—just as easily.

This may happen when a spouse passes away and the remaining spouse continues to live in the property. When the second spouse passes away, an attorney may decide that there needs to be a verification of the property's value at the time of the original spouses' death for some estate regulation.

The value of the property this week will most likely be different than the value five years ago, as markets and the economy change all the time.

One hundred percent of appraisals submitted to lenders go through informal, formal and technical reviews at the Appraisal Management Company level, software systems, national underwriting departments, secondary market entities, local underwriting and others.

Appraisers are constantly asked to review other appraisal reports. Between thirty to fifty percent of all appraisals go through an outside formal appraisal review. Some appraisals may date back a few months while others may go back five years or more, so you never know. If reliable data is available, an appraiser can go as far back in time as needed or until there is no more data.

Have you ever wondered who an appraiser is working for when they walk into your home?

You pay them, so it must be you, right?

Please read on.

Never an Advocate!

Appraisers may provide appraisal services for a variety of different clients, including banks and lenders, the homeowner, an estate, or for a "For Sale by Owner" situation, to name just a few. Please realize that no matter who does the formal hiring, an appraiser cannot and will not assess the value higher or lower than the property's true current value nor ignore any deficiencies or exaggerate them on behalf of any specific party to the report. The data is the data, the house is the house, and the issues are the issues.

In other words, an appraiser may be paid by or work directly for a property owner but the appraiser will never move the appraisal value in any specific direction intentionally. The value opinion and result of the findings must be fact based, without duress, pressure or favoritism to any specific direction or party.

What Should You Know About Your Appraisal Inspection?

The appraiser is a third-party observer whose job is to provide an unbiased and neutral report based on the factual market evidence at a given point in time. The appraiser is never an advocate.

Market Value

The market value is the most probable price which a property should bring in an open and competitive market under all conditions requisite to a fair sale, the buyer and seller each acting prudently, knowledgeably, and assuming the parties are not affected by undue stimulus. Implicit in this definition is the consummation of a sale as of a specified date, and the passing of title from seller to buyer, under conditions whereby:

1) **The buyer and the seller are typically motivated.**

2) **Both parties are well informed or well advised, and each is acting in what he or she considers to be in his or her best interest.**

3) **A reasonable time is allowed for exposure of the property on the open market.**

4) **Payment is made in terms of cash in US dollars or in terms of financial arrangements comparable thereto.**

5) **The price represents the normal consideration for the property sold, unaffected by special or creative financing, or sales concessions granted by anyone associated with the sale.**

When an appraiser is performing an appraisal for federally regulated mortgage purposes using any lender that requires the Fannie Mae and Freddie Mac form 1004/70, the above definitions are what rules the day.

It does not say the most probable HIGHEST price, although that could happen.

It does not say the most probable LOWEST price, although that could happen as well.

It does not say the current price under agreement.

The definition says the most probable price under all conditions in a fair sale.

Why is the Appraiser Coming?

First, let's determine why the appraiser is coming to assess the property.

The reason for the appraisal inspection will control the degree of inspection and the general directions for the research and disclosure needed in the appraisal report.

Is the appraiser coming to perform services on behalf of a refinancer?

Or, perhaps a purchase or sale of the property is involved.

Is the appraiser under the direction of an executor of an estate? Is the appraiser there on behalf of an attorney or court representative requiring an appraisal for valuation purposes?

Is someone interested in buying a "For Sale by Owner" property and wants professional confirmation of the value or some other form of private transaction?

Is someone interested in putting a property on the market and for some reason has limited faith in the real estate agents' opinions of value?

There could be a dozen more reasons why an appraisal is requested, whether it be illness, divorce, part of a business liquidation, bankruptcy, eminent domain, subdivision of property, and so on.

Several of these situations require varying degrees of inspection and reports from physical inspections, "cost to cure" estimates, deeper paper trail research, and varying degrees of support documentation. Some situations require a more in-depth look at the physical and legal property chain than others.

Type of Property

For this quick e-book, a single family home is the type of property discussed throughout the book. This is the most popular type of property in the country and the type most financed through the secondary mortgage market. While multiple family buildings, condos, or any sort of mixed use properties have similar inspection requirements and required reports, they have several differences from single family homes. The single family home is the most prominent type of property owned or desired by most people.

Who is the appraiser's client?

As you now know from the first few pages of this book, the reason why an appraiser assesses your property may involve a dramatic difference in the range of the appraiser's services or variable levels of scrutiny inspection, from a quick walk-through and consultation to an in-depth observation of the property and its components, both inside the house and outside.

The reason why an appraiser is coming to the property will provide a clear indication as to who the client is!

If the appraiser is hired by the executor/executrix of an estate and/or the attorney dealing with settling the estate, the estate is the client and the appraiser is under the control of the executor or attorney regarding what services to perform and at what level.

If the appraiser is coming over as part of a refinancing loan or the sale of a property, the appraiser is there on behalf of the property owner or buyer's loan company. In this scenario neither the seller, the buyer, nor any of the real estate agents are the appraiser's clients. The appraiser does not owe fiduciary responsibilities to any of those parties other than to develop a solid, neutral third-party report. The appraiser's client would be the potential lender.

Should the bank or mortgage lender utilize the services of an appraisal management company (AMC) to process and oversee their appraisal operations, then it gets a little bit cloudier to the public. In this scenario, the AMC is the agent and the bank or mortgage lender is the client/intended user.

There are other cross-pollination scenarios that could be used, but the examples above get the point across for now.

It can be confusing when you hear all this for the first time.

All that you need to remember, regardless of why the appraiser is coming over, is that the appraiser's goal is to inspect and observe the property as a neutral, third-party observer and compare the property to the most similar and most recent properties that have been sold in the area or that are currently on the market.

Types of Financing

- Federal Housing Administration (FHA)
- Housing and Urban Development (HUD)
- United States Department of Agriculture (USDA)
- Rural Housing (RH)
- Conventional Mortgage

For this book, let's work with the most aggressive type of financing inspection and work our way out of trouble. If you prepare yourself and the property for the most in-depth inspection you would have to face, then you should have very little to worry about.

When someone places a home on the sales market, they cannot predict or control who will view the property or what type of financing the buyer will be using. Prepare for the worst and expect the best!

FHA/HUD financing.

This is by far the most in-depth assessment of the property from an appraiser's perspective. I personally do not perform Veterans Administration appraisals and cannot speak about their rules and processes. Please perform your own research as to their guidelines and inspection requirements.

Feel free to check out the **FHA/HUD Handbook 4000.1** and see how vast and comprehensive this manual is. It is truly "big government" documentation with a lot of regulations and oversight.

Observation from the Neighborhood

Ideally, when an appraiser is coming to a property they are already very familiar with the town and the neighborhood and typically the appraiser has performed work in the area before. When an appraiser receives and accepts a new appraisal work order they are by default declaring to the client lender or appraisal management company they are competent for the project at hand, they are competent in the market, and have the tools and knowledge to provide a credible finished report.

Long before the appraiser gets to the property they are making mental notes and should have an idea of what type of area the property is in. Is it business or and commercial? Is it rural, or agricultural? Perhaps it is on a mountain, lake or ocean front? Is it a new subdivision or is the assignment in an inner city or suburb?

As an appraiser drives to the property, they observe the mix and type of property so that they know what comparable properties offer similar surroundings, neighborhood conditions, and appeal, like the subject property. Ideally, similar sales should be taken from the exact location and neighborhood, but in all honesty that rarely happens due to limited inventory.

Observation from the Street

An observation must be made up, down and across the street from the subject property for the type of neighborhood and an appraiser will note any positive or detrimental conditions such as traffic, noise, railway lines, flight paths, gas stations, boarded-up buildings and so on. The appraiser could also note a newer subdivision of more expensive homes, similar and conforming properties, or other neighborhood items. The FHA wants the buyer to limit their long-term liability and maximize their enjoyment of the property and its location and requires more in-depth inspection than a traditional conventional mortgage.

No matter what type of financing is being used to finance a property, an appraiser is on the lookout for all liability issues inside and outside the property. Big, small or in between, if a child or person could get hurt or if the property may become damaged or degraded from a particular situation – it is an appraisers' duty to let the client (the lender or AMC) know about the problem.

Still from the street, an observation is made of the exterior of the property. An appraiser can quickly tell the construction style of the property, its approximate age, if it is a similar age and style to the rest of the neighborhood, the condition of the roof and its approximate age, the condition of the windows, type and condition of the exterior siding materials whether they are stucco, wood, vinyl siding or other materials. A general observation is made of the overall yard maintenance, confirming that the pitch of the land is away from the dwelling, and any obvious easements or encroachments.

The FHA is a Stickler for Peeling Paint.

This is a definite issue and does get commented on often. No part of the exterior of the property can have peeling paint. Not the house, garage, shed, barn or any other structure on the subject lot. If you have any peeling paint, it needs to be scraped and repainted.

There are two reasons for this:

1) Lead paint. If the property was built prior to 1978 and the enactment of the lead paint laws, the property must be scraped and repainted. The ideal time to scrape and paint is when the weather is cooperative and before the appraiser is due to visit the property. Obviously, if it is a just a small section of peeling paint, it is not a big deal. If the whole property has peeling paint it may be a big deal. Either way, if you want to refinance your property or sell to an FHA financing buyer this will need to be addressed.

When the purchase offer is presented to a seller, or the research is done for the refinancing terms, and conditions are stated, there will be a disclosure as to whether the financing program will be FHA or conventional. This book allows everyone to know what is going to happen with the appraisal and plan accordingly to save your time and effort.

2) The second reason the property may need to be scraped and painted is to protect the property from the elements. If raw, untreated wood is left exposed to sun, rain, water or insects the product will deteriorate and break down much faster than if it were treated with stain or paint. This goes back to the long-term enjoyment of the property mentioned earlier. When paint is peeling or nonexistent, dry rot can occur quickly in the wood it should be protecting. This also applies to leaking roofs, termites or carpenter ants—they can do massive damage in a surprisingly short amount of time. If water can get in so can those little pests. There is no long-term enjoyment when these issues take hold of a property.

When the appraiser pulls up in front of a property they may take five minutes to look around the property or general area. The appraiser should be given time and space to observe and make their notes at their own pace. I suggest that you do not rush out to greet them at the sidewalk. There is always plenty of time to say hello and talk. Appraisers realize the homeowner is anxious. The real estate agent needs to be somewhere else. When homeowners or others are present there is a tendency for urgency to get the appraisal done. Allow the appraiser to have the space and time they need to do their job. I personally start on the inside of the property and finish outside for this exact reason. I prefer to initiate contact with the homeowner quickly and allow the real estate agents to move onto their next appointment quickly. Starting inside allows both of those to happen.

By standing on the sidewalk, a trained appraiser can assess the roof style, construction materials and age as mentioned above. They can also tell when a roof is nearing the end of its useful life. Dead giveaways are missing shingles, gaps, rounded edges, noticeable patch jobs, tar filler, or my favorite—the good old blue tarp. The FHA hates blue tarps.

From the sidewalk, most appraisers can tell the type and general age of the exterior siding, whether the property has municipal water, sewer and gas services as seen by observations of the immediate area or by seeing meters on the property's exterior. An appraiser can tell if there are oil filling and ventilation pipes, what kind of electric line is attached to the house, and whether there is a newer electric meter or if it is an outdated line. Do the front stairs have any missing handrails or cracked steps? Are the windows new or old, do any of them have cracked glass or have broken seals, and are they smoky? What type of driveway is present— is it new or old pavement, dirt, stone, and so on?

Obviously, at variable times of the year some items or sections of properties will be hidden by snow, foliage and shrubbery; but most often, in my opinion, most items are observable. Of course, here in New England there are some property styles designed with some flat area elements and flat roofing that may not be observed from the sidewalk. An appraiser will check these areas from inside the property though windows or any porches or decks that allow some visual observance. An appraiser will also look at the ceilings inside the property where these flat areas of roofing are to see if there are any signs of settlement cracks, and current or older staining, which may indicate a failing or recently repaired roof.

An appraiser is required to walk around and take photos of all exterior sides of the property and report what they observe inside most of the outbuildings. In other words, if you are expecting an appraiser have all the rooms and buildings unlocked and ready for observation—sheds, pool houses, barns, boathouses, screen rooms, and so on. Generally, appraisers start on the inside and work their way outside but some appraisers may do the process in reverse. Some reasons for starting inside are to avoid bringing in wet grass, mud, dirt or dog droppings that might get stuck on their shoes. That is considered a courtesy to the property owner. This also helps with the agent or property owners' anxiety to get the inspection started, as well.

Note on Photos; Appraisers are REQUIRED to take many photos inside and outside the property regarding any positive or negative issues observed during the inspection. Prepare for photos to be taken of:

- **All interior rooms.**
- **All four sides of the exterior and outbuildings**
- **Bathrooms, Bedrooms**
- **Kitchens – updated and recent renovations and upgrades… (positive)**
- **Stained ceilings, holes in walls, missing handrails, broken glass (negative)**
- **Attics**
- **Basements, finished or not**
- **Major components – furnace, water tank, electric panel, and so on.**

It is a common courtesy to have the property somewhat cleaned up for viewing but it is not mandatory. Appraisers are looking at structure, components, quality and condition, and hopefully can look past any dirty laundry or clutter, as long as it is not attempting to hide physical neglect and damage.

Be prepared. Fix and repair everything including normal wear and tear not just to meet the building codes and any issues of liability or risk of possible injury before the property goes on the market or before you begin the refinancing process, and definitely before the appraiser gets on site. Do that, and everything will be okay.

Is it a private street or way?

In many areas of the Northeast there are many private streets. These roadways are not accepted as the responsibility of the municipality and they are not always maintained. This will generate several paragraphs of comment in the report and many questions for the owner, agent or community.

- If it is a right of way, what are the terms of use?
- Who is liable if there are damages or injury? Is it a "pass at your Own risk" situation?
- Do police, medical and firefighters respond in that area?
- Who plows the road in the winter?
- Who patches and repairs the potholes or dirt road?
- Who pays for new paving?
- Is there an association to oversee maintenance?
- Are there voluntary or mandatory association fees?
- Is there a written agreement detailing how debts or capital repairs of the roadway and any special assessments are handled?
- Are there any municipal services in the road such as water and sewer lines, and if so who repairs them?

Part of my territory is the City of Worcester, which has approximately 175,000 people. It is the second largest city in Massachusetts next to Boston. This city has hundreds of roads that are private and many have not been maintained in decades.

My area also includes dozens of lakes and ponds with many private roads leading to them, as well as some very rural communities with state or federal forest and wildlife protection areas. Sometimes the roads through those areas are not maintained but they may lead to some residential housing.

Should you come across one of these situations as a buyer, seller or real estate agent, ask the above questions and document what you can so when the appraiser does get there you are ready to proceed.

Finally, Let's Go Inside

We are still basing the inspection on the FHA rules, and if the property can pass this test there should be no problems with conventional types of financing programs and protocols.

One foot inside the door, appraisers will make a general observation as to the overall condition and quality of the property. They will pay attention to consistency as they tour the property. Is it of average condition and quality compared to other homes in the same neighborhood and price range? Is it superior or inferior to others in the neighborhood within the same price range?

During the walk-through appraisers will be looking for water stained ceilings, missing ceiling tiles, large cracks in ceilings, walls or floors, various liability issues, loosely hanging lights or ceiling fans, missing balusters, and other signs of general non-maintenance. If the subject property is not clean and is being minimally maintained, the structure and components of the house most likely not maintained or minimally maintained too.

Are there any smells or odors present? People with pets that are not the best housekeepers often do not know their house smells like feces or urine. How often is the trash taken out? A stranger can walk into a property and smell the trash barrel quickly. These types of situations immediately resonate with the appraiser. If the property owner does not change the litter box and trash barrels frequently, how well are they servicing the furnace, the well, the private sewer system, and are they checking the basement and attic for mold, insects or vermin?

Depending on the type of odor and the source it may take a serious effort to get it out of the walls, floors, drywall and ceiling materials. That impacts the value of the property! No buyer may want the property. If they do, they usually offer much less than the asking price for the expense and inconvenience of hiring a professional cleaning crew to clean and neutralize the odors.

Is the kitchen newer or older? Is it functional and current for today's market? If the kitchen has been completely gutted and remodeled, when did it happen? Within the year? One to five years? Five to fifteen years? This is a direct checkbox in the appraisal software.

Many lenders and Appraisal Management Companies (AMC's) require the appraiser to check for building permits for such a project. Even when professionals do the work they do not always get the permits. In my area of the country, when a contractor enters the Building Department they need to show proof of contractor license, various kinds of insurance, and various job certifications for the project at hand. Some do not have all that. Because of this – and they put it in the contract – the seller has to provide their own permit and hope that will work. Often, no one gets the permits.

The Kitchen

The appraiser is now on the hook with the condition of the kitchen and the date of update because of that little checkbox on the appraisal form. Years later, some minor error could be uncovered during the loan process that requires the file to be looked at again. This may be when it is discovered that there were no permits. It may not even be the appraisers error. Not doing due diligence now might be discovered later and it sometimes tracks back to the appraiser. Enough about that.

An appraiser must now verify that the kitchen is in working order and there are no liability concerns. Appraisers should turn on your water at the faucet and probably wait for hot water to be produced. The appraiser needs to check the lights and a random electrical outlet or two. There will be a random opening of some cabinets doors, drawers, the dishwasher, and maybe a peek under the sink to make sure everything is in good safe order. Taking a step back, the appraiser will take a picture or two of the kitchen, which is also required as part of all appraisal assignments, thanks to the layers of new regulations.

If the homeowner does not want to allow the appraiser to take photos there is no sense in finishing the appraisal inspection. Photos are required

In conclusion,

I trust you are finishing this book with more knowledge and information than when you began reading. If you have questions or concerns, please check my website HubAppraisal.com and my blog posts for other topics that you may be interested in.

If you do not find what you are looking for at my website you can always contact me directly. See the email address below.

Thanks again for reading **WHAT SHOULD YOU KNOW ABOUT YOUR APPRAISAL INSPECTION? And Should You Worry About It?**

If you enjoyed this book, I hope you check out my other works with more coming online soon.

20 Ways Appraisers Can Kill Your Deal!

This book will explain several ways that a property can be marketed or priced incorrectly by agents and homeowners. It describes what appraisers MUST do according to industry requirements and ethics that agents and homeowners may not be aware of for each property. These items lurk in every property, in every town and every deal.

Real Estate Armageddon—Buyers and Sellers Caught in the Crossfire.

This book describes the Great Recession and what happened at the regulatory level that changed the playing field for credit agencies, mortgage companies, mortgage investors and appraisers. Many other industries have also been impacted by this massive legislation. Buyers and sellers are caught in the middle with tighter credit, more stringent verifications, and more oversight due to numerous regulations. What appraisers are required to do is often different than what buyers or seller think. The problem is, no one has explained to the real estate buying and selling public how they may be affected—until now.

You are armed with the knowledge of what appraisers are looking for and what we are charged with doing for every residential appraisal in America that happens to need financing through the secondary mortgage market.

Together, we will get this real estate industry back on track, one deal at a time.

Best regards,

Steven Boucher

HubAppraisal.com

stevedirect@HubAppraisal.com

Disclosures

I am a licensed real estate broker as well as a Certified Residential Appraiser in the State of Massachusetts only. No advice or specific information is intended for any other state.

I am not licensed nor certified to perform Veterans Administration (VA) appraisals, and therefore I have no information or opinions concerning their processes.

This book is intended for education and entertainment purposes, and to provide a general knowledge of the appraisal process and what to expect while an appraiser is on site at a home. This is not a comprehensive discussion of the entire appraisal process and the scope of work of an appraiser.

No client relationship is intended, formed, nor desired from your support and control of this book.

This book is not intended to take the place of a local real estate expert, tax professional, lender or attorney and some sections of the country may have different local practices and methods for the purchase, sale and refinancing of real property. Please seek professionals in your local area concerning your specific situation.

There is a resource page at the end of the book that can direct you to the websites and publications that rule the appraisal industry and what an appraiser does at your specific property.

This book is copyright protected. No reproduction, broadcasting or dissemination can be made in any manner without the express written consent of the author. If you have a PDF version, please do not share the book or link and request that the reader enjoy their own personal copy of the book.

Any company names, symbols and trademarks used in this book are used for reference purposes only; those companies own their respective names, symbols and trademarks.

Cover photo from DepositPhotos.com, used with permission.

RESOURCES

The information and resources below are starting points only. The Federal Government is a large beast with much in the way of paper trail, manuals, regulations and updates since original postings.

If the links below are not active or this is a printed version of the book, please search the Internet for these terms for your specific information or links.

www.HubAppraisal.com

www.FannieMae.com

Fannie selling guide
https://www.fanniemae.com/content/guide/sel120616.pdf

www.FHA.com

FHA/HUD Handbook 4000.1
https://www.hud.gov/program_offices/housing/sfh/handbook_4000-1

Veterans Administration (VA) https://www.veteransunited.com/welcome-pages/va-loan-apply/?src=msn&adg=mvetad&utm_source=bingads&utm_medium=cpc&utm_campaign=lowscores&desc=valoans&st-t=bing-ppc&vt-d=c&k_clickid=2547a773-1693-48ed-affe-abc86bdcf6d0

National Appraiser Registry
https://www.asc.gov/National-Registry/NationalRegistry.aspx

Dodd Frank Act
http://www.cftc.gov/LawRegulation/DoddFrankAct/index.htm

Home Valuation Code of Conduct (HVCC) (NOW SUNSET)
https://en.wikipedia.org/wiki/Home_valuation_code_of_conduct

Appraiser Independence Regulations
https://www.fanniemae.com/content/fact_sheet/appraiser-independence-requirements.pdf

What Should You Know About Your Appraisal Inspection?

What is an Appraisal Management Company
http://www.dol.wa.gov/business/appraisalmgmt/amclaws.html

About the Author

Steven Boucher is a second-generation real estate guy who followed his mother into the business back in the mid-1980's. He continues to serve the public as a traditional listing agent, a buyer's agent, and as a residential certified appraiser. Through the years he has served on various REALTOR® committees at the local and state levels.

Steve has been involved in various levels of public service through the years. He has been a Little League coach and has served on their local Board of Directors. Steve has served on many committees within his local Board of REALTORS® chapter, as a Condominium Board Trustee, and on a few small town committees.

Steve was one of the founding committee members and representatives overseeing the merger of a statewide Multiple Listing Service database conversion. This MLS is now known as Multiple Listing Service - Property Information Network (MLSPIN), which has grown to have major accounts in several states across the country. He is a past president of the local chapter of the Board of REALTORS®, a local REALTOR® of The Year award winner, and a two-time recipient of the local North Central Massachusetts Association of REALTORS® Presidents Award and a two time REMAX® President's Award winner.

Through the years, Steve has been quoted in several publications, and has been a guest speaker on local radio shows and other media outlets. He enjoys every moment possible with his wife and two boys, travel and vacations, an occasional round of golf, fresh water fishing, walking his golden retrievers Bailey and Granger, and camping with family and friends.

His latest hobby is writing various books to provide information about real estate to the public. His intent is to tell the public what regulations the government has put in place, either directly or as a byproduct of the mortgage and appraisal systems and how they impact buyers, sellers and real estate agents when it comes time to buy, sell or refinance a property.

He currently enjoys working on his blog and website HubAppraisal.com as much as possible. Let me know if you have any ideas or topics you want to see covered at *stevedirect@hubappraisal.com*.

For a comprehensive list of Steve's professional accomplishments, please visit **HubAppraisal.com** and check out the **ABOUT** section at the top of the page.

If you are a homeowner, a home buyer, real estate agent or anyone interested in residential real estate, here is a book to put in your collection!

The real estate industry in America has been turned on its head since the Great Recession of 2007.

There are new rules of engagement concerning buying, selling and financing of real estate that you cannot ignore. The federal government is collecting data on tens of millions of properties and keeping them in a master computer database. Appraisers have been researching, detailing and tracking properties and placing them in this database across the country.

The government makes the rules and regulations, and the banking and appraisal industry continue to educate within their own ranks— but who is telling the public how their property or deal may be impacted?

This book is for you!

- **Do you know what appraisers are looking for when they visit your property?**
- **Do you know why appraisers must look in all corners of the property?**
- **Do you know who the appraisers' client is?**
- **Is the appraiser always your advocate to make the deal work?**
- **Market value means the highest value—right?**

The federal regulations and lender requirements do not allow the appraiser to discuss the report or its results with the buyer, seller, or real estate agents while they are in the process of making the appraisal or after the appraisal is completed. However, if you read this book you probably won't have too many questions left.

If you have bought or sold real estate within the last few years, or maybe you are about to buy or sell a property, read this as well as my other books and gain knowledge of what is going on today so that you maximize your money, time and effort to their best potential.

Feel free to visit my website anytime at HubAppraisal.com.

Enjoy the book!

Steve

www.ingramcontent.com/pod-product-compliance
Lightning Source LLC
Chambersburg PA
CBHW040300220526
45473CB00002B/545